very first things to know about

frogs

written by
Patricia Grossman

illustrated by
Karen Barnes

WORKMAN PUBLISHING • NEW YORK

1 A frog is an amphibian.

An amphibian is an animal that can live on land or in water.

Amphibians are cold blooded. Their body temperature does not always stay the same, as ours does. Cold-blooded animals are as warm or as cold as the air or water around them.

2

Toads, newts, and salamanders are also amphibians.

Which of these animals is not an amphibian?

3

2 There are many different kinds of frogs.

Frogs live almost everywhere in the world, except where it is very cold.

The largest frog in the world lives in Africa. It can grow to be more than one foot long and weigh more than six pounds.

The smallest frog lives in Cuba. It is no more than half an inch long. Find the sticker of the teeny-tiny frog on the sticker page. Put it next to the big frog.

Some frogs spend their entire lives in trees. Tree frogs have tiny suction pads on their toes that help them climb up and cling to leaves and branches.

A tomato frog is round and red—just like a tomato!

5

3 Frogs always live near water.

The best place to spot frogs is by a pond, lake, marsh, or swamp.

A frog's skin is smooth and moist. If its skin dries out, so does the inside of the frog's body, and the frog will die.

6

Frogs have smooth, moist skin. Toads have bumpy, dry skin. Which of the animals below is a toad?

4 Frogs like to stick close to home.

A frog's home range is like its neighborhood. In its home range, the frog gets all the things it needs to live.

A frog has lots of reasons to feel safe near home. It knows good places to sleep and to hide from enemies. It also knows where to find the best food.

Some frogs have a home range over 23 times the size of a football field. Others don't move more than five feet from their homes!

Some frogs eat spiders. With your finger, help the frog find a path through the reeds to get to the spider's web.

5 Frogs can change their body temperature.

They do this by moving around their home range. To lower its body temperature, a frog moves from a warm place to a cool one. To raise its body temperature, a frog basks in the sun.

This frog is basking in the sun so that the inside of its body will become warmer. It keeps part of its body in the water so that its skin will not dry out.

10

Find the stickers of the brown striped frogs. Place one in a cool place in the picture. Place the other one in a sunny place.

As winter approaches, most frogs will bury themselves in the mud. There they will sleep, or hibernate, through the cold weather. In springtime, the sun warms the earth and the frogs wake up!

6 Most frogs are green.

The green skin of most frogs helps them hide in their surroundings.

Some frogs don't need to stay hidden. In fact, they want other animals to notice them. Their skin may be bright red, orange, blue, or yellow to warn others that they are poisonous. A bird might eat such a frog and become very sick. That bird will certainly learn never to eat a brightly colored frog again!

Many animals, such as snakes and birds, like to eat frogs. By blending into greenish-colored pond water or among leaves and grass, frogs can avoid their enemies.

12

How many frogs can you find
hidden in this picture?

7 Frogs have long, strong legs.

To move from place to place, frogs walk, swim, skitter, climb, dig…and mostly JUMP!

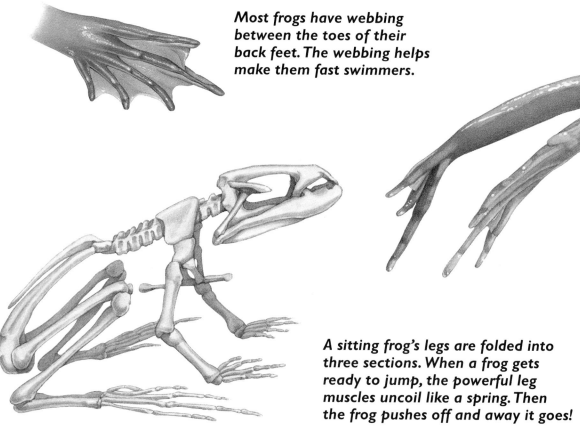

Most frogs have webbing between the toes of their back feet. The webbing helps make them fast swimmers.

A sitting frog's legs are folded into three sections. When a frog gets ready to jump, the powerful leg muscles uncoil like a spring. Then the frog pushes off and away it goes!

14

A frog's powerful back legs allow it to make huge leaps. When a frog jumps, it begins by taking aim at where it wants to go. Then it pushes off with its back legs. Its feet roll off the ground, and it's off! The frog will land on its front legs.

Can you jump like a frog? Can you skitter like a frog?

This frog is skittering. It looks like it is bouncing. Frogs can skitter on water or on land.

8 Frogs have big bulging eyes.

A frog's eyes are set wide apart and bulge out from the top of its head. It can see in front of, to either side of, and even behind itself.

Some frogs' eyes are brilliantly colored red, blue, or green. Others have eyes that shine like gold or silver jewels.

A frog blinks when it swallows. Its eyeballs press down on the food, helping the frog to swallow.

Frogs have an extra set of eyelids. While underwater, they can see through these eyelids, which protect their eyes like swimmers' goggles.

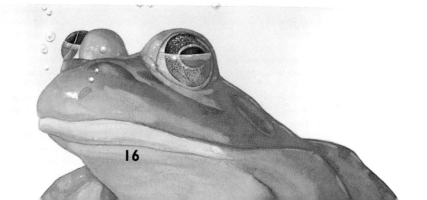

16

Find the sticker of the frog with the bright red eyes. Place it on top of the red flower.

9 Frogs are not picky eaters.

Most frogs will eat whatever they can swallow—including other amphibians and their eggs. Frogs often eat insects, such as flies, mosquitoes, and dragonflies.

Many frogs have a long, sticky tongue for catching food. The tongue stays rolled up in the frog's mouth. When an insect buzzes by, the frog shoots out its tongue—and ZAP!—it catches the insect and pulls it into its mouth.

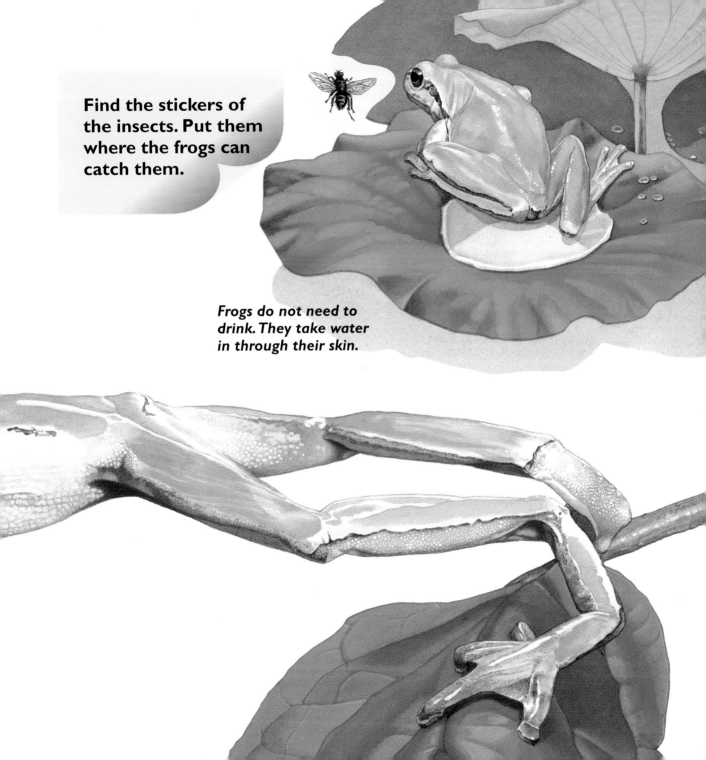

Find the stickers of the insects. Put them where the frogs can catch them.

Frogs do not need to drink. They take water in through their skin.

10 At breeding time, a chorus of frog calls rings out through the air.

Spring or early summer is mating time for frogs. Different kinds of frogs have different kinds of calls. The females listen to the calls of the males to find their own kind of frog.

Male frogs can make calls without opening their mouth because of a vocal sac in their throat.

Some frogs have a pair of vocal sacs on either side of their mouth. When they make the call, the sacs blow up like little balloons.

The female frogs on the left are "listening" to the calls of the males. Match each kind of female frog with the same kind of male frog on the right.

How do frogs hear each other call? Frogs don't have ears that you can see. But behind their eyes are tympanums—eardrums. Sound bounces off each tympanum. Frogs "hear" by feeling the bounce.

II Most female frogs lay their eggs in the water.

As the female lays her eggs, a male sits on her back and spreads sperm on them.

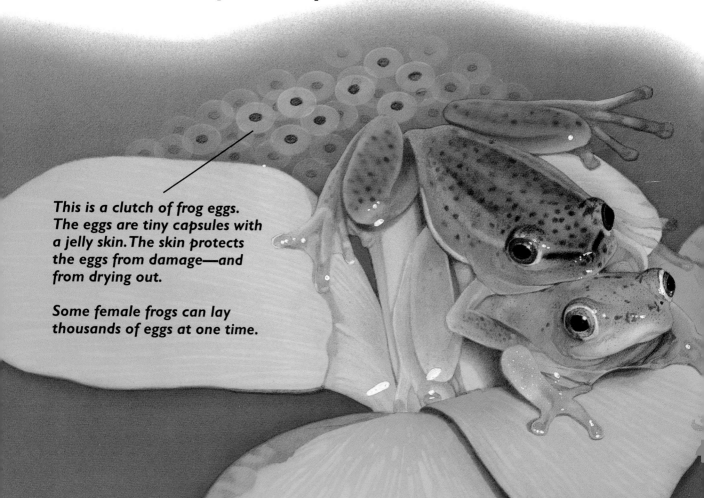

This is a clutch of frog eggs. The eggs are tiny capsules with a jelly skin. The skin protects the eggs from damage—and from drying out.

Some female frogs can lay thousands of eggs at one time.

Most frogs leave their eggs to hatch alone. But there are some frogs that look after their eggs.

Some carry their eggs on their back or in little pockets in their skin.

Can you name some other animals that lay eggs?

Others scoop the eggs into their mouth to protect them until they hatch. When they're grown, the little frogs hop out!

23

12 After a few days, an egg grows into a tadpole.

Tadpoles have long tails and breathe through flaps called gills, the way fish do.

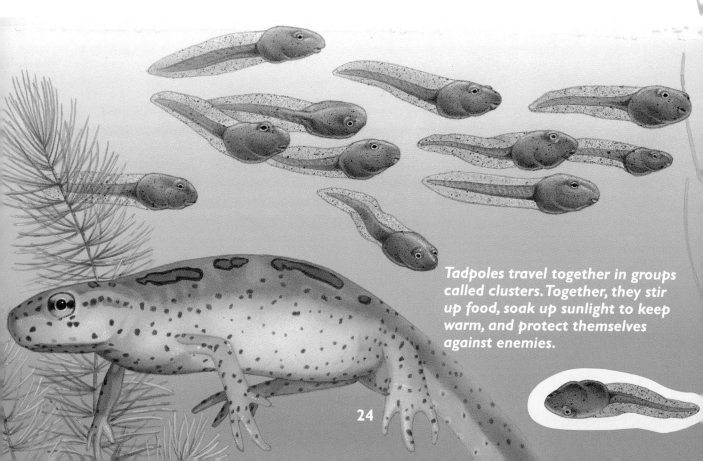

Tadpoles travel together in groups called clusters. Together, they stir up food, soak up sunlight to keep warm, and protect themselves against enemies.

24

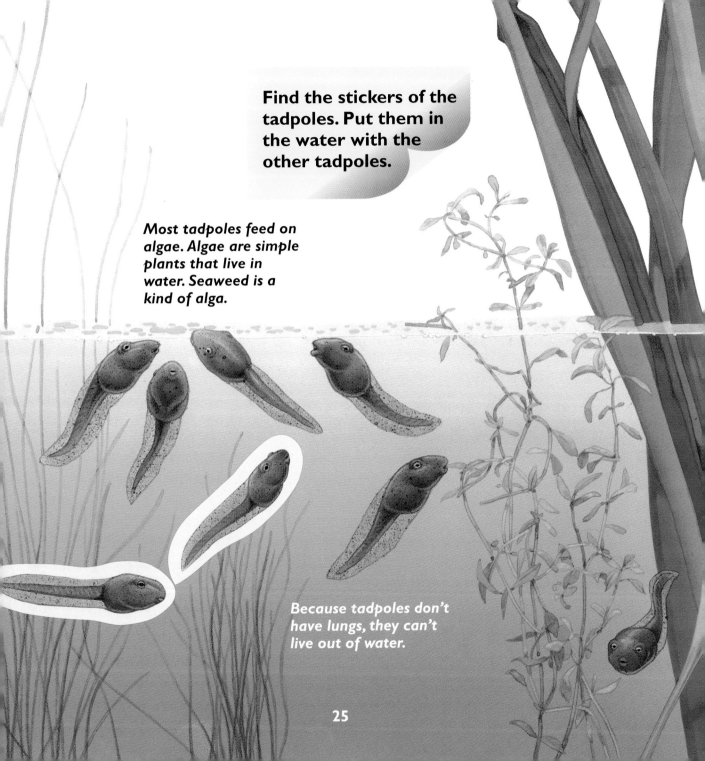

Find the stickers of the tadpoles. Put them in the water with the other tadpoles.

Most tadpoles feed on algae. Algae are simple plants that live in water. Seaweed is a kind of alga.

Because tadpoles don't have lungs, they can't live out of water.

25

13 Finally, tadpoles grow into frogs.

As tadpoles become frogs, their bodies go through many important changes—inside and out.

Tadpoles grow back and front legs. They lose their gills and grow lungs so that they can breathe out of water. They get a true stomach, a spine, and limb bones.

Using the number stickers on the sticker page, put the pictures in the order that tells the story of how a tadpole becomes a frog.

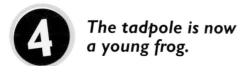
The tadpole is now a young frog.

A young tadpole has a long tail. It looks like a little fish.

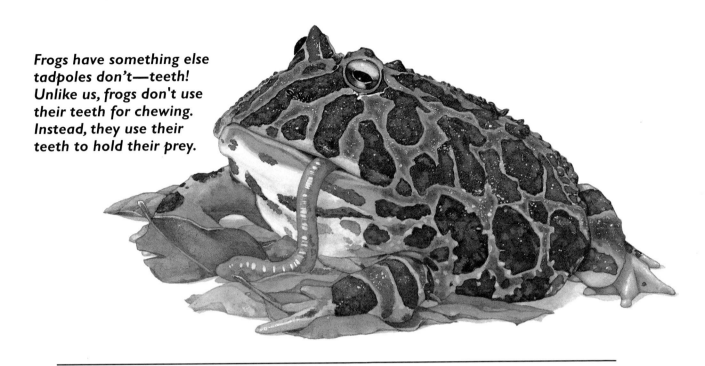

Frogs have something else tadpoles don't—teeth! Unlike us, frogs don't use their teeth for chewing. Instead, they use their teeth to hold their prey.

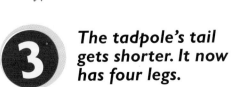

3 *The tadpole's tail gets shorter. It now has four legs.*

2 *The tadpole begins to grow legs.*

14 Frogs defend their home.

Frogs do not like it when other frogs invade their shelters or nests.

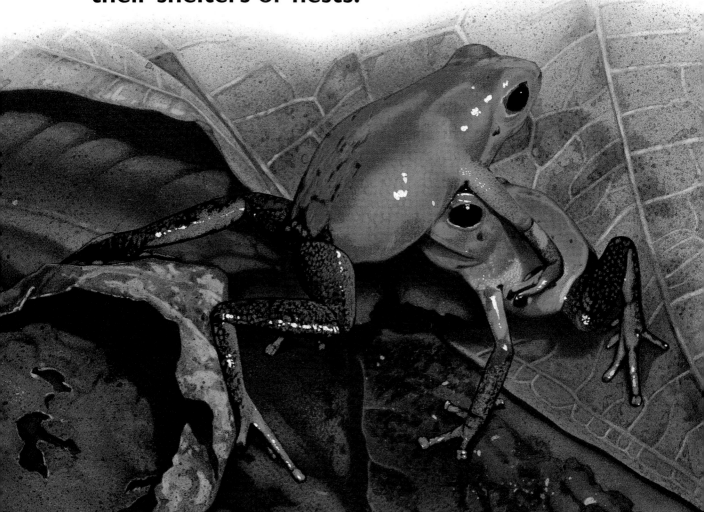

Frogs that live in trees are usually terrific jumpers. Some can leap 40 times their own length!

Some frogs can dig burrows to stay in so that their skin stays moist. They have a knob on their heels that they use like a shovel to scoop up dirt.

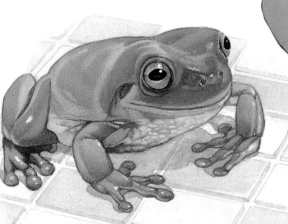

Some frogs even live in people's houses—usually in the bathroom, where it's wet!

On the sticker page, find the sticker of the green spotted frog. Put it on the lily pad.

29

15 Frogs need our help.

People everywhere like to look at frogs because they add beauty to the natural world. Yet they are dying.

Scientists think that pollution—unclean air and water—is one reason frogs are disappearing from their natural habitats.

Find the stickers of the lily pads. Add them to the picture of the frog's home.

What You Can Do to Help Frogs

Tell your friends that frogs are great. Let them know what is dangerous for frogs:
• dirty ponds
• chemicals in the air and on the ground
• too much building in places where frogs live

Answers

Page 3: A fish is not an amphibian.

Page 7: The animal in the bottom left-hand corner is a toad. All the others are frogs.

Page 13: There are seven frogs hidden in the picture.

Pages 26–27: The order of the story is:

1. A young tadpole has a long tail. It looks like a little fish.
2. The tadpole begins to grow legs.
3. The tadpole's tail gets shorter. It now has four legs.
4. The tadpole is now a young frog.

I like
frogs

I know
all about
frogs

I know
all about
frogs

I like
frogs

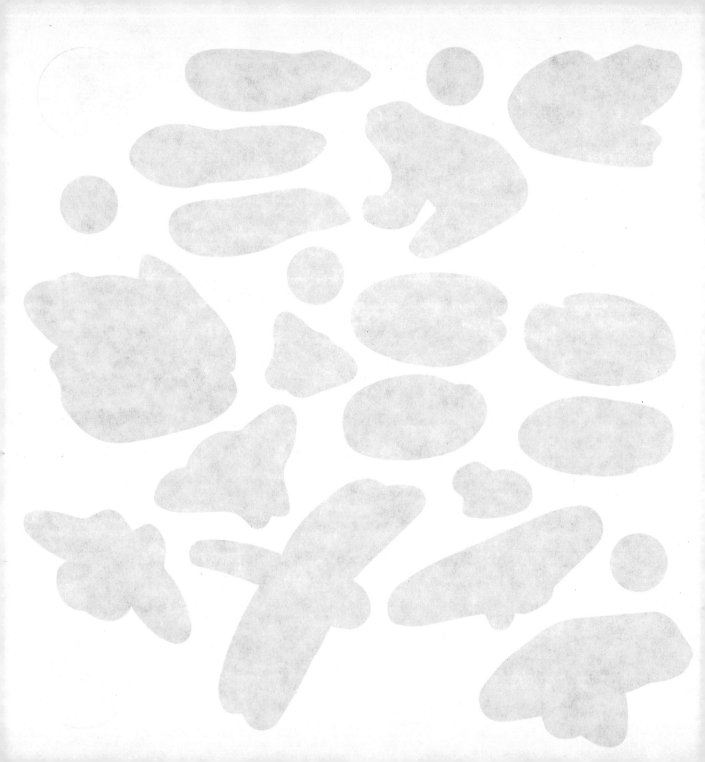

Published by
Workman Publishing Company, Inc.
708 Broadway
New York, NY 10003-9555

www.workmanweb.com

Printed in Singapore

10 9 8 7 6 5 4 3 2 1

Library of Congress Cataloging-in-Publication Data

Grossman, Patricia.
   Very first things to know about frogs/by Patricia Grossman; illustrated by Karen Barnes.
p.   cm.
ISBN 0-7611-0731-2
1. Frogs—Juvenile literature. 2. Toy and movable books—Specimens. [1. Frogs. 2. Toy and movable books.] I. Barnes, Karen, 1962– ill. II. American Museum of Natural History. III. Title. IV. Title: American Museum of Natural History.
QL668.E2G765 1999
597.8—dc21   98-47461
                                                                      CIP
                                                                      AC

Designed by Nancy Loggins Gonzalez and Erica Heitman
With special thanks to David Dickey, Department of Herpetology, AMNH